The Church of All Saints at Newland, traditionally and affectionately known as the 'Cathedral of the Forest', was begun in the early 1200s. At that time the Forest of Dean, the areas between the rivers Severn and Wye, was 'no-man's' territory for the church. The older churches, like Ruardean, English Bicknor, Staunton, St. Briavels, Hewelsfield and Lydney, appeared not to have ventured into the Forest. Concern about this situation was felt by both ecclesiastical and secular authorities leading to the granting of land, around AD1200, to be cleared for the foundation of a church. King John appointed Robert of Wakering as first Rector in 1216.

The original, probably rather small, building was expanded during the next two hundred years to the size and shape of the present church. A major restoration in the 1860s widened the chancel arch and slightly raised the roof of the nave. On the west wall the marks left by successive alterations to the height of the nave are visible. The village of Newland did not exist before the clearing was made in the Forest and the church built. The surrounding houses were built in subsequent years – mainly comprising large 'country houses' for important families who lived elsewhere for most of the year.

In addition two groups of Almshouses for local aged persons in financial need, were founded. One group, by Edward Bell, was built in conjunction with his Grammar School at Newland – now a private house within the churchyard. The second group of almshouses were built by William Jones, a wealthy London merchant who came from Newland. He also founded another group of almshouses and a Grammar School at Monmouth, which are run by the Haberdasher's Company.

Robert de Wakering, first Rector in 1216

The South Aisle

The main entrance to the church is by the south door, through a porch which originally had a room above used for meetings and a local school. On the walls of this porch are fragments of carvings discovered during the nineteenth century restoration. They are the few remaining indications of the carvings which were in the church before the banning and destruction of such things, partly during the Reformation but mainly during the Puritan revolution of the seventeenth century.

The south aisle contains many items of historic interest. There are a number of wall monuments to local families, including the Coster family who were important in the metal-working industry, particularly copper and brass in this parish at Redbrook and in Bristol during the seventeenth and eighteenth centuries. At the entrance to the St. Edward Chapel, lies the free standing table-tomb of Sir John Joce and his wife, owner of the original Clearwell Castle and lands which he gave to his son-in-law Robert Greyndour. During the 1863 restoration the tomb was unfortunately 'tidied up ' by local stonemasons – much to the annoyance of the consultant architect, William White.

The tomb of Sir John and Lady Joce

In the west end of this south aisle, near the font, is the unusual effigy of John Wyrall, dated 1457. John Wyrall held an important position in the government of the Forest of Dean – being a 'Forester at Fee'. This effigy was brought in from the churchyard in the 1950s to prevent further erosion. His clothes and hairstyle provide valuable information about the dress of that period.

This example is typical of black lacquered "Shield Dial" Tavern Clocks, probably made between 1750-1780. This type of lacquering is also known as "japanning".

The symbolism of the eagle as a lectern derived from the belief that the bird was capable of staring into the sun and that Christians similarly were able to gaze unflinchingly at the revelation of the divine word.

The St Edward or Probyn Chapel

The window in this chapel is by Kempe and was dedicated in 1898 to Georgiana Dighton and her children by her husband. It depicts, in the centre, the Virgin Mary and the infant Jesus, with St. Anne and her daughter, the young Virgin Mary, on one side and St. Elizabeth and her young son, John the Baptist.

The St Edward Chapel is small and crammed with wall monuments. The most magnificent, displacing the original altar, is that of Sir Edmund Probyn who became Lord Chief Baron of the Exchequer in 1741.

His coat of arms showing an Ostrich's Head erased holding in its beak a key gave rise to the name of the Ostrich Inn situated opposite the lych gate.

Close by the St. Edward Chapel and the Joce tomb is an unusual stained glass window in memory of Charles John Brickdale, a naval officer from a Newland family, who was born in 1819 and was killed on board H.M.S. Comus in action off Point Obligado, on the River Parana in South America, on 20th November 1845. He was buried on the shores of the Parana. It depicts in roundels, the name of 'Comus' and 'Parana' and an illustration of the battle.

Next to the Brickdale window is the Headmasters board of Bell's Grammar School which was founded in Newland and is linked with the adjacent chapel of St. John and St. Nicholas

Beneath the Brickdale window is a raised stone slab bearing an incised figure of a bowman. Re-cut in the nineteenth century this may represent a seventeenth-century member of the Wyrall family wearing the symbols of office of 'Bow-Bearer' to the Crown.

The St John And St Nicholas Chapel

The St John and St Nicholas Chapel is linked to the sanctuary by the work of a local craftsman – Andrew Pyke who designed the furniture in memory of a Newland parishioner who did much for the church during the twentieth century.
The importance of the chapel over the centuries explains the various names it has been called. As the 'Clearwell Chapel' it reflected the fact that it was built by Sir John Joce, owner of the original castle at Clearwell. Later generations called it the 'Dunraven Chapel' . Various memorials and hatchments on the walls relate to the Dunraven family and their relations, notably the Wyndham and Quinn families. Also called the 'Greyndour Chapel' this refers to their family foundation which provided an early type of grammar school adjacent to the church.
The famous 'Miners Brass' is inserted in a slab with the Baynham name inscribed. This brass is unusual in being in relief. It depicts a miner in working garb with his tools and his lighted candle which was held in place by sticking it into a lump of clay attached to a stick gripped in his mouth. Its origins are unknown; reputedly it was returned to the church in the early nineteenth century.

The Ludlam window

The Fortescue-Brickdale family renovated the chapel about 1912. The reredos was designed and painted by an eminent artist and member of the family, Eleanor, now regarded as an important member of the 'Birmingham School' which carried on the traditions of Pre-Raphaelitism. The reredos, which could be classified as distinctly 'feminist', depicts the Virgin Mary with the Christ child, flanked, in separate panels, by her cousins Elizabeth with her son John the Baptist, and her mother Anne with her distaff.

The Chancel And Sanctuary

The chancel and sanctuary apparently underwent various alterations between the commencement of the building of the church and its comple tion about two hundred years later. The chancel arch has been considerably widened and the step before the sanctuary step may indicate the eastern end of the original church where the sanctuary rails are to-day. The siting of the altar or Holy Table in many churches changed from being against the east wall of the sanctuary to being in the centre of the chancel when Puritan beliefs took precedence. During the Oxford Movement in the nineteenth century the altar was reinstated at the east end of the sanctuary. Provincial churches, in the main, did not have choirs or choir-stalls until the nineteenth century; the chancel, or 'side chapels', were the place for worship for normal services. The spacious sanctuary, with its elegant black and white marble tiles, is beyond the altar or sanctuary rails. The rails were not part of church furnishings until well after this church was built. The great East Window has imposing nineteenth-century stained glass depicting the Resurrection and the Ascension with the Virtues inhabiting the upper sections. In front of this window is the large High Altar upon which are the wooden cross and candlesticks in contrasting dark and light wood designed and made in recent years by a local craftsman, Andrew Pyke, trained in the continuing tradition of the Arts & Crafts Movement.

The East End

The Lady Chapel, so called because it is dedicated to the Virgin Mary the mother of Jesus, is rich in furnishings and monuments. This chapel was founded in the fourteenth century, probably by the Chinn family who owned a nearby mansion called 'Highmeadow'. This chapel provided 'Morrow Mass' priests to go into the Forest to the small and scattered iron mines, and later coal mines, to take the Sacraments and Scriptures, and comfort where necessary. The magnificent Perpendicular east window was re-discovered in the nineteenth century when an eighteenth-century addition, probably a vestry, was taken down. The nineteenth-century stained glass in this window depicts the raising of Lazarus flanked by Lazarus's sisters, Martha and Mary.

In the south-west corner of this chapel is the remains of a spiral staircase which is one of the oldest sections of the church. Originally it was extended upward to connect with a large rood-screen. Whether this screen was across the present chancel arch or led to a screen at the present entrance to the Lady Chapel is not certain. Near this staircase is a magnificent late fourteenth-century effigy of a priest in full Eucharistic vestments; the type of vestments re-introduced into the Church of England in the nineteenth century.